P9-CCO-593

War Planes

Revised and Updated

Long-Range Bombers
The B-1B Lancers

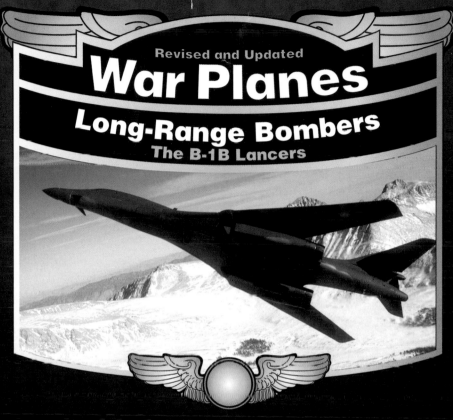

by Michael and Gladys Green

Consultant:
Raymond L. Puffer, PhD, Historian
Air Force Flight Test Center
Edwards Air Force Base, California

Cuyahoga Falls Library
Cuyahoga Falls, Ohio

Capstone
press

Mankato, Minnesota

Edge Books are published by Capstone Press,
151 Good Counsel Drive, P.O. Box 669, Mankato, Minnesota 56002.
www.capstonepress.com

Copyright © 2008 by Capstone Press, a Capstone Publishers company.
All rights reserved. No part of this publication may be reproduced in whole
or in part, or stored in a retrieval system, or transmitted in any form or by any
means, electronic, mechanical, photocopying, recording, or otherwise, without
written permission of the publisher. For information regarding permission,
write to Capstone Press, 151 Good Counsel Drive, P.O. Box 669, Dept. R,
Mankato, Minnesota 56002.
Printed in the United States of America

Library of Congress Cataloging-in-Publication Data
Green, Michael, 1952–
    Long-range bombers : the B-1B Lancers / by Michael and Gladys Green — Rev.
and updated.
       p. cm. — (Edge books. War planes)
    Includes bibliographical references and index.
    ISBN-13: 978-1-4296-1318-7 (hardcover)
    ISBN-10: 1-4296-1318-1 (hardcover)
    1. B-1 bomber — Juvenile literature. I. Green, Gladys, 1954– II. Title. III. Series.
UG1242.B6G72 2008
623.74'63 — dc22   2007031334

Summary: Introduces the B-1B Lancers, their specifications, equipment, weapons,
     missions, and future in the Air Force.

Editorial Credits
Carrie A. Braulick, editor; Jo Miller, photo researcher; Katy Kudela, revised
     edition editor; Kyle Grenz, revised edition designer

Photo Credits
Defense Visual Information Center, 1, 17, 22, 25, 29
Photo by Ted Carlson/Fotodynamics, 4, 7, 9, 10, 13, 18–19, 20
Photri-Microstock, 26
Wikipedia, public-domain image, cover

1 2 3 4 5 6 13 12 11 10 09 08

Table of Contents

The B-1B in Action

Learn about
- B-1B development
- B-1B design
- Radar systems

A U.S. Air Force B-1B Lancer flies over an enemy country at night. The B-1B's crew locates its target. Doors at the bottom of the aircraft open, and a large object drops from the plane. The strange object falls apart in the air, and dozens of small bombs seek out their targets. An enemy missile base is destroyed.

Enemy radar systems locate the bomber. One enemy missile flies toward the B-1B. A computer in the B-1B releases a small decoy that confuses the missile's guidance system and the missile misses the bomber.

An enemy pilot then fires a heat-seeking guided missile at the B-1B. The B-1B launches bright, hot flares. The missile follows the flares instead of the bomber. The B-1B crew returns safely to its air base.

Building the B-1B

In 1965, the Air Force wanted a new long-range bomber to replace its outdated B-52 Stratofortress bomber. In 1974, aircraft manufacturer Rockwell International built four test models of a new supersonic bomber that could fly very high and fast. These planes were called B-1As. But the B-1As were never built. Government officials canceled the project in 1977. They did not believe the planes were needed.

By 1981, the government decided it needed a different version of the B-1A. Rockwell International built an improved model of the B-1A called the B-1B. The Air Force ordered more than 100 B-1Bs. In 1985, the Air Force received its first model.

The Air Force has more than 70 B-1Bs in service.

About the B-1B

The Air Force depends on B-1B crews to perform missions anywhere in the world on short notice. The B-1B is designed to travel long distances to reach a target. The B-1B's bomb bays allow it to carry a number of weapons.

Pilots often fly the B-1B low to the ground during missions. Enemy radar systems cannot easily detect planes flying close to the ground.

The B-1B has features to help crewmembers perform their missions. A defensive countermeasures system protects the aircraft from enemy weapons. Radar equipment helps crewmembers aim weapons and keep track of their surroundings.

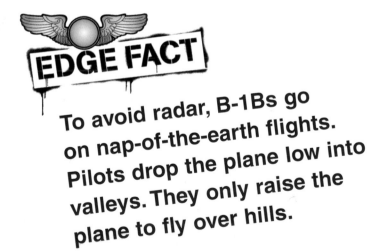

EDGE FACT

To avoid radar, B-1Bs go on nap-of-the-earth flights. Pilots drop the plane low into valleys. They only raise the plane to fly over hills.

Inside the B-1B

Learn about

- VG wings
- Countermeasures system
- Flying the B-1B

The B-1B can weigh up to 477,000 pounds (216,634 kilograms) when loaded with weapons and equipment. It has the largest payload of any Air Force bomber. The B-1B has a sturdy frame and strong landing gear to handle the weight.

The B-1B must carry a large payload over long distances. Tankers can refuel the plane during flight. The B-1B crew then can continue to fly instead of landing to refuel.

Adjustable Wings

The wings of most planes do not move. But the B-1B's wings can move forward or backward. They are called variable-geometry (VG) wings.

A B-1B pilot uses a lever to move the wings of the plane. This lever makes it easy for the pilot to choose the exact wing angle.

For takeoffs and landings, B-1B pilots point the wings straight out. This position helps the aircraft quickly climb and fall.

Pilots often point the wings toward the tail during flight. This wing position reduces **drag**. The B-1B can fly faster with its wings swept back than it can with the wings straight out.

Powerful Engines

Four large jet engines power the B-1B. Each engine can produce about 30,000 pounds (13,600 kilograms) of thrust. This force pushes the aircraft through the air.

drag — the force created when air strikes a moving object

The jet engines on the B-1B help it travel quickly.

The B-1B's engines give it a top speed of more than 900 miles (1,448 kilometers) per hour. But B-1B pilots usually fly the plane about 550 miles (900 kilometers) per hour to save fuel.

Countermeasures System

The AN/ALQ-161A countermeasures system protects the B-1B from enemy weapons. The system warns the crew if radar-directed missiles approach the plane's rear. It may send out a decoy that confuses the enemy's missile guidance system. The missile then flies between the plane and the decoy instead of hitting the plane. The AN/ALQ-161A's radar jammer also can send out electronic signals to prevent enemy radar systems from working properly.

The AN/ALQ-161A sometimes releases strips of metal called **chaff**. Each metal strip reflects radar energy to the station to confuse the radar system.

The AN/ALQ-161A can send out flares. The flares help protect the B-1B from heat-seeking missiles. These missiles are designed to follow a plane's hot engine exhaust. The missiles may follow the flares instead of the plane's exhaust.

chaff — strips of metal foil dropped by an aircraft to confuse enemy radar

B-1B Specifications

Function:	Long-range bomber
Manufacturer:	Rockwell International/Boeing
Deployed:	1985
Length:	146 feet (44.5 meters)
Wingspan:	137 feet (41.8 meters) with wings extended forward
	79 feet (24.1 meters) with wings folded backward
Height:	34 feet (10.4 meters)
Weight:	477,000 pounds (216,634 kilograms)
Payload:	75,000 pounds (34,020 kilograms)
Engine:	Four General Electric F101-GE-102 jet engines
Speed:	900 miles (1,448 kilometers) per hour
Range:	7,500 miles (12,070 kilometers); unlimited with in-flight refueling

Navigational and Control Systems

Pilots fly the B-1B at fast speeds close to the ground. The aircraft could easily crash into the ground or other objects. The B-1B has an autopilot system to help the plane fly low.

A computer is connected to a terrain-following radar (TFR) system in the aircraft's nose. Pilots look at the cockpit's radar screen to see objects in their flight path. The computer automatically flies the aircraft around the objects.

Air currents close to the ground can make the B-1B's ride bumpy. The B-1B has a Structural Mode Control System (SMCS). Two small wings called vanes are located in front of the plane's cockpit. The vanes are connected to a computer. The computer detects rough air and adjusts the vanes to keep the plane level.

Four crewmembers fly in the B-1B. The pilot and mission commander sit at the front of the cockpit. They operate the control systems to fly the plane.

EDGE FACT

Flying aboard a B-1B can feel like riding a roller coaster. The plane's SMCS makes flying easier for the crew.

The SMCS keeps the B-1B level during flight.

The offensive systems operator (OSO) and defensive systems operator (DSO) sit in the rear of the cockpit. The OSO uses the plane's radar system to aim and release weapons. The DSO controls the B-1B's countermeasures system.

wing

tail

engines

bomb bay

engines

wing

The B-1B Bomber

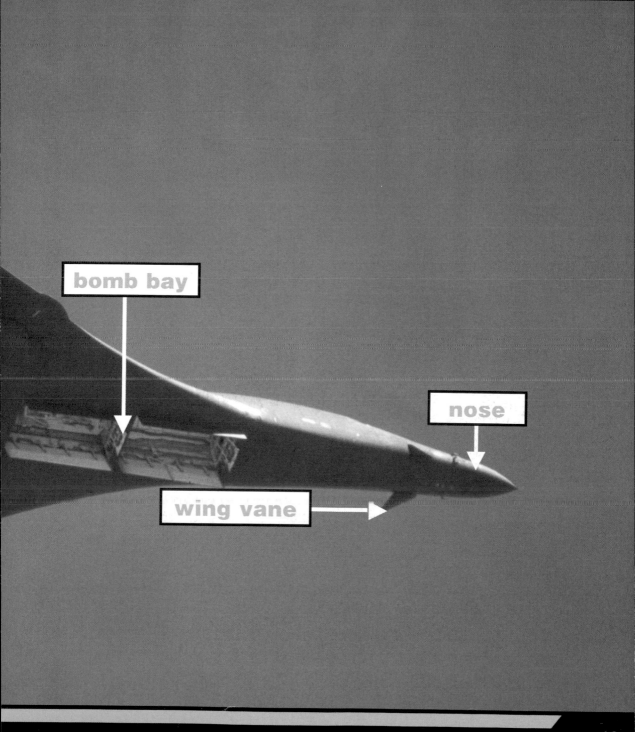

bomb bay

nose

wing vane

Weapons and Tactics

Learn about

- B-1B bombs
- JDAMs
- Cluster bombs

The B-1B carries mainly air-to-ground weapons. It also can carry weapons to destroy enemy ships. The B-1B carries its weapons in three large storage areas called bomb bays. The bays are located near the center of the plane's body. The B-1B can carry about 75,000 pounds (34,020 kilograms) inside the bomb bays.

Some of the B-1B's bombs weigh 500 pounds (225 kilograms).

Bombs

The B-1B often carries unguided bombs. These bombs are not guided by electronic systems. The B-1B can carry 84 unguided bombs that each weigh 500 pounds (225 kilograms).

The B-1B also can carry 24 unguided bombs that each weigh 2,000 pounds (900 kilograms). Crewmembers use these bombs to destroy targets such as large buildings and bridges.

JDAMs

Crewmembers use the Joint Direct Attack Munition (JDAM). The JDAM includes a kit that fits over the tail of an unguided bomb. It adds a satellite receiver and a motor to the bomb.

Spacecraft called satellites orbit earth and guide JDAMs. Satellite-guided weapons can accurately hit targets even in bad weather conditions.

EDGE FACT

Both the Air Force and the Navy use smart bombs such as the JDAM.

Other Weapons

The B-1B can carry up to 30 cluster bombs or CBU-97 Sensor Fuzed Weapons. Both types of bombs hold smaller bombs called **submunitions**. Smaller bombs can destroy targets spread out in a large area better than other bombs can.

A sensor sets off a small charge in cluster bombs and CBU-97s as they fall over targets. Submunitions then drop from the bombs and explode when they hit an object. Each cluster bomb can release about 200 submunitions. A cluster bomb can affect an area about 910,000 square feet (84,539 square meters). The CBU-97 releases 10 submunitions. Each CBU-97 can affect an area about 600,000 square feet (55,740 square meters).

submunition — a small bomb carried by a larger weapon and released as the weapon approaches its target

Serving the Military

Learn about
- Recent B-1B missions
- Improvements
- Future Air Force plans

Many people believe the B-1B is too expensive to operate. They believe the Air Force should retire it. The Air Force spends millions of dollars updating the planes. But many Air Force officials believe the B-1B is an important part of the military. Pilots have flown it on many successful missions. In 1999, B-1B crews took part in Operation Allied Force in southern Europe. Militaries involved in this operation wanted to force Yugoslavia's military out of a region called Kosovo.

In 2001, B-1B pilots performed missions during Operation Enduring Freedom. This operation targeted terrorists in the country of Afghanistan. B-1B crews dropped more than 3 million pounds (1.4 million kilograms) of weapons during the missions.

Improvements

The Air Force often improves B-1Bs. In 1993, the Air Force began the Conventional Mission Upgrade Program. The Air Force has improved the B-1B's communication, navigation, and radar jamming systems through this program. In 2003, the Air Force added a new towed decoy system to the B-1B. It is called the AN/ALE-50.

Manufacturers are developing new bombs for the B-1B as part of the upgrade program. Raytheon is producing the satellite-guided AGM-154 Joint Standoff Weapon (JSOW). The JSOW releases submunitions. It has a range of about 40 miles (64 kilometers).

The B-1B carries JSOWs similar to these.

The B-1B also will carry the Joint Air-to-Surface Standoff Missile (JASSM). Lockheed Martin is producing this missile. The JASSM has a range of about 1 mile (1.6 kilometers).

Air Force officials may soon retire some B-1Bs. But they plan to keep the bombers in service until about 2038. The Air Force depends on its B-1Bs to perform missions throughout the world.

GLOSSARY

chaff (CHAF) — strips of metal foil dropped by an aircraft to confuse enemy radar

drag (DRAG) — the force created when air strikes a moving object; drag slows down moving objects.

exhaust (eg-ZAWST) — heated air leaving a jet engine

payload (PAY-lohd) — the total weight of the equipment carried by an airplane

radar (RAY-dar) — equipment that uses radio waves to locate and guide objects

submunition (sub-myoo-NI-shuhn) — a small bomb carried by a larger weapon and released as the weapon approaches its target

tanker (TANG-kur) — an airplane equipped with tanks for carrying liquids; tankers can refuel other planes during flight.

thrust (THRUHST) — the force created by a jet engine; thrust pushes an airplane forward.

READ MORE

Casil, Amy Sterling. *The B-1 Lancer.* U.S. Warplanes. New York: Rosen, 2003.

Hamilton, John. *The Air Force.* Defending the Nation. Edina, Minn.: Abdo, 2007.

Stone, Lynn M. *B-1B Lancer.* Fighting Forces in the Air. Vero Beach, Fla.: Rourke, 2005.

INTERNET SITES

FactHound offers a safe, fun way to find Internet sites related to this book. All of the sites on FactHound have been researched by our staff.

Here's how:
1. Visit *www.facthound.com*
2. Choose your grade level.
3. Type in this book ID **1429613181** for age-appropriate sites. You may also browse subjects by clicking on letters, or by clicking on pictures and words.
4. Click on the **Fetch It** button.

FactHound will fetch the best sites for you!

INDEX